AURORA AMERICANA

PRINCETON SERIES OF CONTEMPORARY POETS

Susan Stewart, *series editor*

For other titles in the Princeton Series of Contemporary Poets see the end of this volume.

AURORA AMERICANA

Poems

Myronn Hardy

PRINCETON UNIVERSITY PRESS
Princeton and Oxford

Published by Princeton University Press
41 William Street, Princeton, New Jersey 08540
99 Banbury Road, Oxford OX2 6JX

press.princeton.edu

All Rights Reserved

Library of Congress Cataloging-in-Publication Data

Names: Hardy, Myronn, author.
Title: Aurora Americana: poems / Myronn Hardy.
Description: Princeton; Oxford: Princeton University Press, [2023] |
    Series: Princeton Series of Contemporary Poets |
    Includes bibliographical references.
Identifiers: LCCN 2023001461 (print) | LCCN 2023001462 (ebook) |
    ISBN 9780691250571 (paperback) | ISBN 9780691252537 (hardback) |
    ISBN 9780691253671 (ebook)
Subjects: LCGFT: Poetry.
Classification: LCC PS3608.A7285 A96 2023 (print) | LCC PS3608.A7285 (ebook) |
    DDC 811/.6—dc23/eng/20230130
LC record available at https://lccn.loc.gov/2023001461
LC ebook record available at https://lccn.loc.gov/2023001462

British Library Cataloging-in-Publication Data is available

Editorial: Anne Savarese and James Collier
Production Editorial: Theresa Liu
Text and Cover Design: Pamela L. Schnitter
Production: Lauren Reese
Publicity: Jodi Price and Carmen Jimenez
Copyeditor: Jodi Beder

Cover image: *The End of the Beginning*, Alexander "Skunder" Boghossian, 1937–2003, born Ethiopia. Oil on canvas. H x W: 122.3 x 169.2 x 3.8 cm (48 3/16 × 66 5/8 × 1 1/2 in.) 91-18-2. Museum purchase. © 1972–1973 Aida Boghossian. Photograph by Franko Khoury. National Museum of African Art / Smithsonian Institution.

This book has been composed in Adobe Garamond Pro and ScalaSans

10 9 8 7 6 5 4 3 2 1

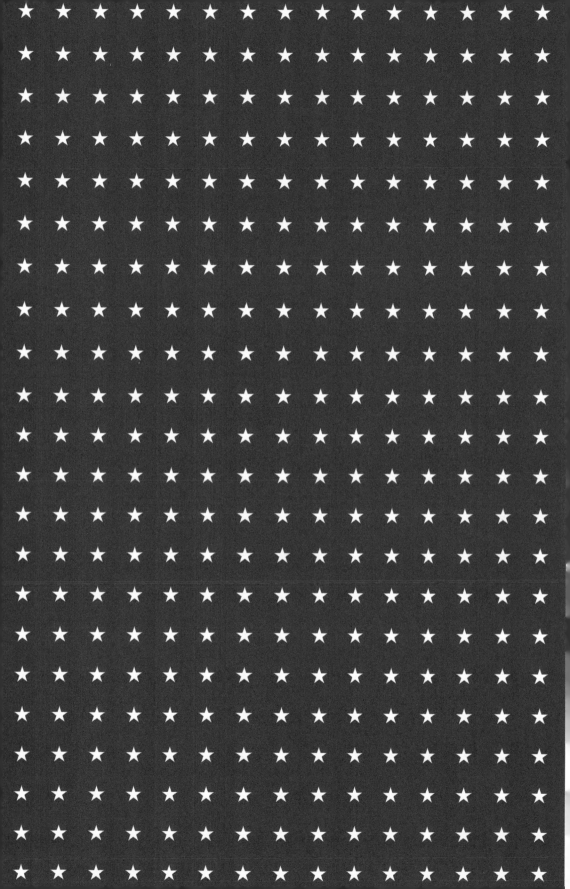

Contents

★   ★   ★

There is another world
but it is inside this one.
—PAUL ÉLUARD

What does it mean to protest suffering,
as distinct from acknowledging it?
—SUSAN SONTAG

For Mom

always

AURORA AMERICANA

AURORA AMERICANA

The most interesting thing about emptiness
is that it is preceded by fullness.

—JOSEPH BRODSKY

1.

She leaves me outside among yellowing
aspens. Hemlock branches
discarded   dying on this iced clod.

Corms in the ground whiten waiting for another snow.
Fissured face   the skin of me fissured.
The leather of a carriage no longer

fit to front a manor with sequoia moldings
or doors carved in California   shipped
to Louisiana to shut in that house.

Made for another girl now dead. Her mother
made me out of that tatty carriage-seat leather.
Made me as she evoked her mother's

country dissolved in seawater.
I'm the leavings of seawater left cold.
Forgotten in cold.

Forgotten in this northern place.
They've forgotten what I've not.
The dark is without forgetting.

That woman filled me with pink
cotton   that annual spell when
cotton explodes that gaudy hue.

I'm holding time in the dark   waiting
for the dappling of sky.
I hear them.

I know them.
They'll do the thing that wrecks.
They're unworthy of themselves.

This knowledge wrecks.
But a jester?
That jester?

His brashness   a theory of this land.
A quality encouraged for navigation.
I'm not protected.

Cold   unprotected at night.
Solitary at night inducing
more creasing   more

staining as they stain themselves   as
they beg for regression. As
they beg for the nineteenth

century   the century I was made.
Hold the clock's clicking.
Turn it back   make-make America.

She leaves me to see this night.
To see blue televisions through windows.
To hear raucous commentary.

She leaves me to see this night   to
freeze among the frozen.
There's yellow in the trees tonight.

The girl who leaves me wears
a yellow dress.
Her boots are white.

2.

I voted for snow   frost   crystals.
I see them falling.
I've been falling into myself.

I see myself with myself.
I hold my own hand as I walk through snow.
I walk with my twin.

I wish for a country of twins.
Our slacks are patterned with stars.
We're partisans.

We believe in the belief.
There's only one belief.
There's only one nation.

We're the founders of the nation.
Our blood for this nation.
Our blood in this nation is the nation.

We see it in sunset.
All that we've given is sunset.
We aspire to what the billionaire has built.

The lavishness of pink marble
wild in our sleep.
We want what he has.

We believe what he has is his.
We believe his dream is American.
We believe his reality can be ours.

We believe in oligarchy   ours.
We're waiting for the chalice   that goddess's
slow pouring of shine.

But that frozen doll frightens me.
I'm walking away but I keep
craning toward it.

Its face of creature   its darkness
on that which is frozen.
I leave it there.

They're left. They're not me.
We voted for snow   its perpetual system.
Radically radical we voted.

3.

He wanted me away.
I want him away from
that public house.

In his dream   I'm the boy
locked in steel.
There's water in his dream.

I sink.
He saw my hands reaching
from the steel until they didn't.

I was a boy.
We were boys.
He wanted to kill the boy.

He wanted the boy dead
in steel   quickly
a man in steel not of it.

We became men in steel.
In the paper   he bought our
capture   shouted execution.

Years in steel.
The sky's steel here.
It's cold here.

My daughter is here.
I want her to play.
Be a good girl   play.

I want him away from
that public house.
How is he a choice?

Up in Michigan   near Lake
Superior waiting for spirals   funnels
of jade   ginger light.

This dawn is near but which dawn?
Which will be created?
So cold here in this north.

The north wouldn't protect.
When has it ever protected?
When has this place protected me?

But I'm trying to protect my
north   my daughter
in winter-white boots.

The breeze isn't silent.
I want him away from
that public house.

I stare skyward yet I see
the glare of televisions.
My daughter's fingers are cold.

4.

My father is afraid
but he doesn't say it.
I came in from playing to see

him   to be around him.
His hands are colder than snow.
His hands are chapped.

Why are your hands so cold?
The past was cold. I don't want
the past to permit what may come.

What?
He embraces me. The world
is around me.

Snow   strange   I'm waiting
for something I don't understand.
Will you wait for me?

I'm here   forever here   around.
He's angry at the television.
The blue of the television

is what's inside him.
If I could open him   an abrupt
door I could open   step into

the blue   step into brightness
burning my eyes.
I'm quickly blind

within the blue of my father.
He mentions   *jester.*
He mentions   *clown.*

He mentions   *criminal.*
He mentions   *killer.*
Where's your doll?

I have left her without knowing.
Left her freezing   left her among snow
without protection.

I have to find her.
Go find her.
Bring her inside.

My coat like skin   fake fur on skin.
I'm running back to save
the one I forgot.

How could I forget her?
She has been forgotten before
but I didn't want to forget.

Everything tall   green
heavy with whiteness.
My father is upset even

when there are auroras
above him   above me   above
this country.

5.

It isn't dawn when she returns.
But I thought if there will
be a return it will happen at dawn

when America shows what she
hides   what she whispers   what
she denies in conversation   what

she calls crazy in public.
I know this place.
I know its makers.

Those with soft
hands   rough   always
rough within. They smile

yet hide tundras.
Within them tundras with paths
lined with wet spikes.

Something dead on the spikes.
Something dying on the spikes.
She's kissing me.

I'm being carried   kissed
among firs   snow blowing.
They will do it.

They have done it before.
Regression   angry at the lie
they can't keep from questioning.

I'm loved by a little girl
who knows nothing of me.
I want her father to scream.

If he doesn't   he may die early.
He may leave his daughter early.
So many men leave their daughters early.

Don't be shocked.
Perhaps you've left your daughter?
Fissured face   the skin of me fissured.

Does she know what these fissures hold?
Does she know what she holds?
Does she know what

her father's holding?
What he doesn't say
when he sees her   when

he sees the jester?
His hands are over his ears.
She sees him on the porch

as if holding his head together.
It could erupt.
It could combust   St. Helens.

Dust   fire   smoke like
that mountain.
We're all combustible.

But first   implosion.
The birches within us falling.
Not the leaves in autumn

but the trees themselves   falling.
Paper bark   mangled.
The hidden thump   that

crash beneath ivory cages   skin.
This isn't greatness.
This isn't noble.

A terrible enactment in
the dark   the light   the cold.
She drops me on the porch

to hold her father's face.
Hold me.
Hold.

Hold.
Hold.
Hold.

6.

I'm cold here.
Waiting as blue hits my face.
I've made a fire.

Crackle.
Crackle.
My son burns marshmallows.

They're gooey on graham
crackers. Chocolate melts
on sweet sandwiches.

The auroras are rare.
I want my son to see the auroras   that
which is possible in sky.

This was my place as a boy.
This was where my parents took
me to say this is ours.

This piece of it is ours.
We feed ducks bread.
But what bread feeds us now?

There's poison in the bread.
We're losing.
So much poison   poison

to survive but we
are surviving without ourselves.
Save us.

Save us with your wealth.
Save us with the way you make wealth.
Fire what's killing us. Burn the ground.

Wall us in. We're being killed.
They're killing us.
Aurora.

Aurora my love   I'm
waiting for Aurora.
When you come   will we be saved?

Auroras in that sky swirl in the cold.
O beautiful for spacious skies
For amber waves of . . . .

7.

This is reality?
This is a reality star?
His reality isn't our

reality but they believe it can be.
Their reality is fake.
Their false reality exists in their minds.

They're convinced of their reality.
Some realities are based in trickery.
They want their reality.

But how can their reality be true? The nonexistent true
only when reality is hostage. They've swaddled reality
in deception making it *true*. Oh   he changed my reality   that

reality of innocence to criminal.
My reality became prison.
His fake reality made my reality   my

reality of childhood to manhood fugacious.
My reality of custody   trial   conviction
was his   the country's made reality.

The reality is   it is almost dawn.
The reality is   my daughter is sleeping.
The reality is   this place is now more dangerous for her.

The reality is   auroras are stunning.
I'm staring at the reality of stunning auroras.
I'm in a reality stunned.

8.

Dawn gleams.
In my dream   my father is content.
He's unworried.

He's lifting me into cloying light.
I'm wearing a dress of light he has made.
So many are waving at us.

We're waving back.
A chalice of light is poured
into the sky.

Snow is falling.
Snow the color of light is falling
but we aren't cold.

SOLEMNITY

At the mosque's entrance   3:30 a.m.   Syrian
women beg wearing black gloves.
Your father's grandmother was Syrian

before the country was ash.
Before the government turned
to kill its people.

What incites that internal blaze?
What says   *it is me I will take*
or not me   but those whom I claim?

We're claimed after meditation.
We're walking an empty street
after pretending to play drums.

After I recognize the heather in air
after we swim in a pool surrounded by azaleas
after your mother smiles observing us

after we sleep in her house   fields
of sunflowers. I'm on a bus
watching them sway. I'm forgetting

the distance   the inevitable loss
I will hold warm as snow whitens the green.
What will you hold?

What will you see beyond your hands?
Streets lined with jacarandas
that morph to pines   to a self beneath

ice that wolves trample silently?
Someone still begs.
Someone still believes in our

innate generosity.
You're waiting for me but refuse to say it.
You believe in returns.

You believe in the planet's roundness.
You believe in gravity's inaudible assurance.
You believe in what I doubt.

FANON'S COUNTRY

Did Fanon watch a flock of pigeons
up from ground then to the green
terracotta where they perched then paced
making themselves propellers?
Was this their confusion with space?
The low   high of it   the strangeness
of swooping? Did he ever consider
himself being where he was strange?
Algeria strange for him?
Or was that home?
Is being conscious the way to hold
a place? Become it?
Pigeons with white undersides   his
translucent palms he presses against
each other after the writing day ends.
The mountains are lavish with cedars.
He watches a friend carry a rod
of bread through the square.
He will not tear it among pigeons
but among family when
they eat green soup never
questioning where they are.

MISSILES

The leisurely way we stroll from school.
The cool around us in the gray as we
wait for sun   as we anticipate bean
soup   bread   green apples   tea.
A woman looks through the kitchen
window seeing specks of yellow   a gathering
of missiles   an aftermath before the slain.
Give me the slain.
Allow me to wash them.
Dress them in cotton.
I have dressed myself in cotton.
I'm clean.
We stare at her not knowing
what she sees.
See
me   we
think.
Turn to
see
me.

THE RAGE: 11 AUGUST 2017

Up from darkness   the darkness
of this earth warm beneath their feet.

Casting canary on pale skin   pale
shirts   the paleness of their ignorance.

Rage as ignorance roaring in the dark.
Darkness as cotton masks but I illuminate obscurity.

This time   born from kerosene.
Charismatically contained to torch not free

to take leaves   things bound beneath
dead skins in Opernplatz.

How I towered   towered in darkness.
The rage of it.

The rage.
The rage.

But these are the same people
obsessed with themselves.

The falseness of themselves
imagined through generations.

Nothing spun from grace
only breath   whim   ailment.

I illuminate bronze weathered
blue   an inventor of this atrocity.

Oh beautiful ideas.
Oh beautiful land.

This was never for all.
We're luminous about the inventor.

This séance of intent   ascend   ascend.
Winged beings beneath him.

Winged beings in a room where he slept
with a child he owned.

I was there too   trembling in glass.
At Shadwell too   consuming his house.

They're consuming this house.
Our house is burning.

THE HISS

You hear the hiss of something unseen.
You stand outside the house built in a previous century.
A woman occupies the parlor.
She waits on the sofa observing timid shadows
marred with holes. Hear the marching   the horror
of hooves against hardened dirt.
There was joy in that house   around
the table when steam blossomed from stew.
You were in that room.
Loved someone in that room.
You hear the hiss of it without warning   its
nearness to ear.
Close your eyes to pull the world
in   the world that almost was.

BLUE CIRCLES

Give me the circle where blue falls.
The rarity of it from satellite
when we touch that which
beats   the rhythm
that sustains.
How we forget that syncopation.
How we are so bound to it   its blue
within arteries   its circles.
Its blue over a trombonist
before he stops   before he
receives ovation.
Its blue over the one
who doesn't see you.
The one you see near
a mother   the veil
about her   a kind
of spring in a blue bottle.

BLUE NEON

The world dissolves in tea.
A blue sphere of sugar among leaves
leaching chlorophyll   zinc.

What I know is more than I should.
The battle within the battle.
The wind's audacious drag of sweet

thorn leaves against pavement.
The boy I was walking home from school
at lunchtime   my blue neon sneakers

a hovering device imagined.
My eyes closed.
A ringing.

Blue neon arrows shoot from my back.
I'm the nucleus of a circle of arrows.
Up.

Up.
Up.
Away.

CITY OF SAUDADE

A different musician performs in the city of saudade.
Different policemen stare at us in the city of saudade
as jacarandas sway near a pink building.
Plump men lug sacks of celeriac into the restaurant.
A customer speaks to a burned-out light bulb.
He's predicting his death. Nothing brutal other than
the brutality of ending   no longer smelling the sea.
We regret those losses of fragrance.
The peonies we gave to girls who chose us the first time.
They chose us with only stems not blossoms wild with sugar.
I want to return   to play in that station when a poet
slings his bag of books over his shoulder.
His hair   juniper   shaped into a sphere.
What he knows will hold us here.

CONSIDERATION

Ask them when they surround me.
When light from the vaulted window
strikes my face   will they mean what
they will do? Is it a decree
given by general   president   god?
Will they regret?
Will they consider their own inquest?
If so   what will they feel?
Considerate responses could end this wild
reign   could open the stars on our flag
exposing their gleaming ores.

PARADE

That thin horse is forced to pull
the gaudy carriage.

The lines about its stomach suggest
a finite universe which we're bound.

Which we abuse like the horse
almost blind   ill-fed   its

back full of welts.
The jester wants a military parade.

Tanks in streets grinding misery
into our own.

The power we give him grinding
us to flex unrecognizable.

Something metallic that burns
smelling of the feathers we tear

away because there is nothing else.
He's in a carriage drawn by angry horses.

He throws bullion to angry
people yet they remain angry.

Perhaps they aren't angry with
him but whom they've become?

Those wild selves in mirrors   on
television   seen through

surveillance cameras.
The jester is saluting them

as his looters continue to toss
what they've taken.

PASTIME

Remove the stones with the chiseled numbers.

We'll forget them   only see dandelions   trimmed

juniper   two gazebos where we'll sit to ponder ourselves.

Not the war   the plague that ceased them   that

allows bulbs to fissure clavicles with violet.

Tyrannical noise.

We're obsessed with noise but not the tyrant

who exposes witlessness like teeth.

But his profundity is his knowledge

of our forgetting. It's past time

in this bountiful land.

SUGAR SNAP PEAS FOR FANNIE LOU HAMER

They have poisoned the cattle   the pigs.
Flies swarm the Delta   the decomposing mounds.
They take the eyes first.

Biting into them as if lychees   embryonic.
She wasn't devastated by sight   the nothing she'd have.
Earth crushed into palm.

The possession of land means life.
Grow sugar snap peas in Sunflower
County   everywhere you can.

Think of them in ground as they
beat   beat the ground in you.
Or the sea   the foam of it ringing ankles.

You're carrying a plastic sack of gutted sardines
because a friend asked you to bring fish to her house.
She will show you how to season   serve with tomatoes.

You will show her how to slice onions in silence.

THE EMPEROR OF TERRACOTTA ROOFS
CONFRONTS THE JESTER

He's standing at the highest point of the roof.
That beautiful blue thing stares
at that high cerulean. Sirens   emergency
sirens spin red on tops of cars   vans   on
walls where glass has been broken.

He's bewildered rearing his head to scream.
The emperor screams for what has
fallen   for what has become
material   cold   stitched together
with something barbed.

Down from the top   he's careful.
His pale blue feet clutching those tiles   he
prances on the roof's edge balancing his
train of feathers   each possessing an eye   each
seeing what it sees despite the agony of gaze.

What has erupted continues to kill.
The jester is juggling glass spheres
on the balcony. He watches
the emperor turn   stare as if to strike.
The emperor calls.

The blush of his tongue   the tunnel of his throat
something soft against that serrated sound.
Sirens   sirens as spheres shatter
on limestone   on moving cars that keep moving.
We only have the air in our hands.

AMERICANA: A BECOMING

The boys jumped into the river.
Swam to the bottom knowing
of the ship weighted with
emeralds   their green garden.
You told me   *they are poor* despite
what sparkles from them.
Our pace was slow   like acquiring
knowledge. Unlike the speedboat
that scattered water.
You said   *I'm black too*   as if
you'd been hidden   camouflaged
as another   my acuity dull.
Now you tell me something else.
When I tell you what I see   what you
told me before   you sham shock.
What has three years in America done?
What has a gluttonous
beach town   beach state
of alligators   swampland   fraudulent
referenda   jester upon jester made you
believe you should discard?
Made you discard yourself?

THE TURNING

The satellites have been turned
off   turned away from

other satellites.
The world is over.

The world without eyes turns
to the glare within itself.

The burning.
We burn.

He burns us.
He is burning.

Barren honey locusts' branches
are dark beneath his skin.

Branches as dark veins writhe
in translucence.

The world is atomic.
He is obese in atmosphere.

Crude over destabilized
mountains   whirlpools of dead perch.

Even the evil among us
see him in air circling.

See the man they have made
king killing us all.

THE MOTH IN THE DRYER

Among the cyclone of my shirts   I
see your beige flutter. The paper
you are among dyed cotton   drying.

I open the dryer door but you don't
emerge from that artificial heat   that
fatal swirl of dead plants.

Fumbling through the shirts
you are nowhere until the door
is closed   the spinning.

You flutter in the eye of it.
A thing struggling   struggle itself
among that which will kill.

Outside   the pungency of pesticides
sprayed the previous night makes me cough.
Your wings have detached.

You're swirling with the cyclone
as a boy blows a sphere of thistles
detaching into a field

of Queen Anne's lace.
He's alone but speaks
as if he were not.

The swifts see him as they
dash   assail the moths remaining.
What airplanes sprayed over

soy fields killed my aunt
Jennie Lee. We're
so small here.

IMPOSSIBILITY

You didn't expect to fall asleep
but you did briefly in the pew.
Briefly in the dim quiet
before the brief ballad of priests.

No myrrh that day
but always marble   gold   reminders
of what survives within the earth.
A woman from Angola walks near you

with a squirt bottle.
Her gaze determines you were dragged inside.
Seraphs did it because you wanted
to recall Catholic school

because you were lost.
Because someone you don't know
will bring you a sack of grapes   a
bottle of water.

Because you don't know if your
love is near or wants to see you.
You will leave in a month.
You attempt to hold that slippery thing

but understand you will fail.
Impossible snow   impossible
sea frozen over in shards.
Someone will meet you wearing

shards that will melt.
She will tell you the story of ice.

CANCELED FLIGHTS: AN ODYSSEY

The fogginess of where   why.
Those nights sprawled on airport chairs.
You're not lost but they've lost you.
Are they trying to keep you or keep you out?
The country where you've lived presents itself as vile.
A snipped telephone line when you were speaking of injustice.
The return to a mind you hoped was over but there it was.

Yell to the ceiling subtly severing.
Your suit   all of your underwear   the statue
with one hundred rusty nails all gone.
Browse the bookstore shelves after
returning from Atlanta sleepless.
Unravel the snail like cinnamon roll.
It's butter with your green tea.

You love this café.
It wanted you to see it before leaving.
Sit here.
Read the book you bought.
Recall what you wrote here.
Recall the woman you kissed here.
Recall who you were.

DEMOCRACY AMERICANA

Forgive us for bells we heard   those we didn't.
Forgive us for ourselves as ourselves.
Forgive us for causes   effects.
Forgive us for loving the thing we say we don't.
Forgive us for unloving the thing we say we do.
Forgive us for seeing   not seeing.
Forgive us for hoping for the thing we couldn't say.
Forgive us for whispers.
Forgive us for disbelief.
Forgive us for shock.
Forgive us for hiding everything.
Forgive us for imprudence.
Forgive us for ferocity.
Forgive us for obliteration.
Forgive us for slyness.
Forgive us for getting what we want.

We are what we want.

LEVITATION

The argument   its ferocity
disassembles your arms to specters that hold
your almost-mind from levitation   reconnecting
to space   the dust   the charge.

Those glowing pieces will eventually dim.
But you have stopped wandering   wallowing
in what has left you crumb because you weren't
expecting to see Prince stenciled to granite.

The word *love* written in cursive   crimson
on the beige building. You were the boy
roused to see the sky the color
he describes rain. Over the birches   that color

the same as priests' vestments during Advent.
His stenciled face in Paris after you'd lost her gleam.
After you'd bought mushroom crepes   you
spoke to the shop owner in Arabic.

He recited all of the Arabic words for *love*.
He could see your loss of it.
He watched you leave hoping your
real arms would return.

Prince lost a son.
Prince gave money to women who lost sons.
Perhaps Prince was lost?
Perhaps Prince lost someone in Paris?

But you aren't lost now.
You're back in Detroit.
. . . we have gathered here today
Let's go crazy . . .

A song raucous in your childhood
home when you were the only one there.
The air swiftly strange.
You turn to the river shimmering.

You're under something that shimmers.

CRISIS

Demigods   self-determined   deter their worshippers from
aligning with logic or intuition. With this understanding   please realize the
word *crisis* comes from the Greek although Latinized   meaning a *change*.
Now this change refers to that in the cycle of a disease. Our disease is our crisis.

FANON'S BANANIA 1953

To realize you are not.
That fall from a self
they claimed was yours.

You were of it until you saw
posters on city walls.
Your reflection distorted

but to them it was you.
The red cap   the same red as lips.
The confection   the same brown as skin.

As a student   Senghor wanted
to rip away each poster.
His fingers would bleed.

So what?
Me on stone.
Stolen me on stone.

You turned away
from those shellacked walls.
The red handkerchief

in your hands was something
alive   something
you carried to Algeria.

Minds exploding in a building
where you were made healer.
Years of healing   heal me

as posters peel from stone.

FANON IN TUNIS   AFTER TUNIS

Speak of exile in a dank room.
Write that word on damp paper
before opening blue shutters.
Before leaving the apartment for the street

before coughing after your first sip of coffee
before recalling the creak. I'm asking why
the world has become this. Silent sirens   this
epidemic   this twisting of a wretched thing.

This was perhaps your question
but you had an answer.
Spoke to it at the University
then   that evening surprised by

the purple scatterings on the streets.
So fragile   strange even
this life against stone.
You're sipping coffee watching

people pass each other.
After you've passed   I'm
watching people pass each other
yet I'm sipping tea.

You loved poetry.
You brought others
to hear Césaire.
Now   the poet is perpetually exiled.

Now   but not then.
Now   because of then.
Now   because of now.
Now   because we're now.

FANON CONSIDERS THE JESTER

But he isn't that unique.
This is what bubbles within them   us

then into the air   into the soil.
Tendrils twirl from the soil.

Bougainvillea twirls over a white wall.
I lean against the wall.

I see white despite closed eyes.
This is the burden   the tumbling

back   the willful unknowing.
The hand you thought dead rising

from an opened grave
hot around a gun.

The tendrils with purple
blossoms   red

blossoms twist about me.
My neck   our necks aren't safe.

FANON IN BETHESDA

We are nothing on earth if we are not, first of all, slaves of a cause, the
cause of the people, the cause of justice, the cause of liberty.

—FRANTZ FANON

No frangipani branches against the window.
No red blossoms other than those blooming
through what is being destroyed.
Call me Ibrahim for my protection   yours.

What are they doing to me?
I will continue to fight the glare I see   that
pouring in of it   this dawn.
This country is anti-me   anti-us.

I'm hovering over craggy
mountains   my skin ashen with frost.
I've been wounded in a dusty field.
But what I say will be said again.

I will say it without a mouth.
Holes where roots burrow   force
themselves through clay   calcium   slate.
What is beneath lingers   waits to erupt.

GAZA GHAZAL: BLUE DISSENT

They have swathed the blue baby in our flag to carry her
to the cemetery. The fury of noise lacerates.

Blue because of wild sky   it's falling over men with doves.
Towers grow from burning tires   above noise lacerates.

The lightning in these mountains perks night to morning. Afraid
the car will slip from the road yet no doves   noise lacerates.

White smoke performs like lightning. They are in danger if struck.
The earth in Gaza burns. We burn   no love   noise lacerates.

They are holding tires. They want to return   to circle
back like water   clean water yet above noise lacerates.

I don't want to end on this wet road. I don't want to drown.
I want to see what grows after rain   after noise lacerates.

After the blue veil drops   a woman wearing a skirt
    jacket   hair the same tint as wheat declares   *noise lacerates.*

The seal   dedication   the same tawny as are the tiles.
This consecrated core   the fury of noise lacerates.

MISS ALGERIA AFTER VIEWING
THE BATTLE OF ALGIERS

for Khadija Ben Hamou

Beneath the grapes was a gun   retrieved   triggered
to end a colonialist.
But perhaps not an end

at all   merely an induced sleep   coma
or was it there before?
Before that most recent

invasion   the one they fought   their
remains in sand   remains in soil.
They breathe remains.

Khadija carries a basket
of grapes to her mother.
They spread the grapes

on the kitchen table.
They eat until their skin is that of grapes.
Their country is afraid of grapes   afraid

of southern grapes they
deem they are not.
They crush grapes to wine.

OBLIVION

*If the, and I use this term extremely loosely, 'leadership' of Louisiana
wishes to, in a Nazi-ish fashion, burn books or destroy historical
monuments of OUR HISTORY, they should be LYNCHED!*

—MISSISSIPPI STATE REPRESENTATIVE KARL OLIVER

You speak of destruction.
Poplars   pointing to poplars not buckeyes or hackberries.
What dangles from them?
Pale fingers as ice   the chill surging.
What they have hoisted   moored   drawn taut.
That blue they felt that broke them.
Blue veins   bluer.
The   sway.
The   sway.
Blue   breeze.
Blue   water
lapping the Delta   Mexico   Cuba.
Who dissolves whom?
Whose sores continue to leak?
I think it wiser.
Bronze   to ground   to storage   to gallery.
Robert E. Lee saw destruction
in certain cenotaphs.
The way they wound the ripped.
But you want more wounds   perpetual wounding.
You feel wounded without wounding.
Satchmo on the radio   his pitch.
The perfume of formaldehyde   this
wounding   last wounding

the cloud of it in that white room   naked in that room.
                                            The dead can see.
                                            The dead can see you.
                                            You are calling them dead.

MUHAMMAD ALI AT LA LUNA
BUT NOT THE BOXER

The flashing florescent bulbs can't
interrupt our obsession with screens.
We're speaking to them until a car flashes by.

Until a sycamore branch sways too low.
Until a friend returns after surgery well but weak.
Our other friend's name is Muhammad Ali

but he isn't a boxer.
His hair is slicked back as if slain.
Dark men on the ground but we can't see the ground.

There are too many dead.
I keep thinking of the dead.
Walking with them as I sleep.

Muhammad Ali is shaking.
He is trying to tell me something about myself.
Something not pondered   not trampled by hooves.

He points at me but I see Joe Frazier fall.
Hear the thump.
Women's feet against the earth   palm against palm.

War warring despite that rhythm within.
Muhammad Ali has a poster of
Muhammad Ali on his ruddy bedroom wall.

He realizes what we assume he does not.

MY LEBANESE FRIEND BUYS BLUE
CONTACTS IN BEIRUT

Because all the girls in his high school
had crushes on the Nordic exchange student.
Because they compared his hair to corn silk   moon
rays   something poetic   something
they sensed they weren't.
Because he felt he could   had to buy some of it.
In that store for something plastic   something
blue   a cold ocean.
He could show those girls a place to wade
where they'd turn briefly   be distracted briefly
from what they'd absorbed.
The shrapnel lodged   lodging within.
The blasts are ceaseless.
In Tunisia   a surgeon will blue your irises.
Scoop out mineral for water.
The jester wants Norwegians to fill a continent.
The rest are banned   sent back
or sentenced   steel as wire or rods.
My Lebanese friend is walking
around Beirut wearing blue contact lenses.
His mother asks if he's blind.

NO LONGER

But we don't know each other.
Haven't swapped three sentences.
That corner where you scream
demanding money is a vacuum
where bitter oranges quietly
sour on thin boughs.
We are no longer friends?
But we never were.
The words "longer"   "friends"
I don't deem you understand.
"Longer" means time.
"Friends" compel time
we never made.
We know nothing of each other.
I assume you inhabit a margin   a
different one than my own.
You know all in this town of addicts.
You take from those not from this town.
The town knows what you take.
The town knows your leg was taken from you.
Knows you hide steel in its place.
On that corner every morning
shouting for the luck you
never had   *no longer friends.*
Never friends.
Never.

ON VALENTINE'S DAY A POOL IN ALEPPO

But you taste without reluctance that which the sky released
on Tuesday. Face submerged   the cold clarity the world no longer sees.
You see the gouged gypsum floor   your face as beast
but you taste without reluctance that which the sky released.
Ochre shirt over ochre skin   the world you imagine hasn't ceased.
From your palms grow small pale blossoms you've seen in trees
but you taste without reluctance that which the sky released
on Tuesday. Face submerged   the cold clarity the world no longer sees.

THE CHAMPIONS

The black players of France are also black players
for the entire black world.

—GRÉGORY PIERROT

Too much rain over Moscow but a prime minister
kisses the champions on their foreheads.
His dark suit slick with water.

The champions are soaked as if they've

floated from the sea but they are jubilant.
So many Africans are floating in the sea.
Are drowning among plastic   whitening coral.
These champions know of the drowning   the desperation

that comes from besieged land   those
who wish them besieged.
Not them   not today   but.
How cannons blast gold foil squares

that stick to skin   ground.
It's my last Saturday in Morocco.
We're praising victory.
How much gold are we worth?

THE PANTHER IN LISBON

after Chadwick Boseman

Arrive when the theater is black.
Your eyes aren't adapting but you can see
the blue lights of the stairs blur.

Dots of blue where you hope not to tumble.
You're not on screen   not the show
but you're black.

You're black in a black room
where those on screen are black.
You're saying farewell to that white country.

That theater is filled with white people.
It's Saturday night.
As you're oohing   the stranger

near you offers popcorn.
That afternoon you ate grilled octopus   your
friends had cod   pineapple.

You walked through baroque
churches   their grotesque gold like a sea
animal   tentacled   greedy as disease.

Those Brazilian mines sucked sterile.
After the film you discuss it   mugs
of beer in your hands.

The stranger tells you of his return
from Beira   red carnations on stone streets.
This old city was new.

Farewell to it in the dark.
Your dark soles on white stone.
What snarls before you?

What stares back as you wave?

THE JESTER LIVES IN THE PALE HOUSE
BUILT BY THE ENSLAVED

Smiling.

He's on television pretending to be glorious.
He's making others redden with it.
They're in.

Believe they are.
They understand him.
They've always understood
that that pale house was

theirs   his   theirs   his.
The capital   the resolution for it
made from two slave states
makes the jester   smile.

We're made of this bounty of bodies.
We're obese with them.
That black child born
in that house knows the jester's   smile.

Watches him with a woman who loathes.
Hears her say   *he is the opposite of glorious. My God. My God.*
That ghost child sits on the table with the bronze bust
of King hoping it won't melt   hoping its maker

won't melt from the sky.

THE SLUR DURING RAMADAN

I shake an acquaintance's hand before
he begins bargaining for lamb shanks.
The butcher speaks that slur   points to me.

The acquaintance tells the butcher   *no   he
is a friend.* I pretend not to understand
buying loquats   sour cherries   peaches.

Holy   holy   holy month   my mouth
is dry. The butcher chops meat.
Everything is a thing.

Nothing is divine.
I've heard the slur before   while
buying soup in the north.

Its articulation
interrupted the rhythm of waves.
It flooded synapses where ghost

ships were trailed by hammerheads
in water more sunset   so much dead food.
Beige faces on television smeared

darker brown. They're mocking braids   Afros
to make an audience laugh. They're laughing
severely   their history of trade severe.

How is this month holy?
How did Ahmed Zaki negotiate himself?
How did Cairo negotiate him?

The screen   the screen
there was no negotiation.
That slurred man is adored.

That man was already himself.

THIS SCHEME OF MAKING

That purple flag flaps beneath the palm.
Near the fountain a couple waits for language.
We're all waiting   leaning against

moss   ivy consuming walls.
Walls made from centuries
of sediment   bird dung   fossilized

crocus bulbs. Such walls buttressed
a scheme of which we're dazed   the thing
that blazed these criminals to power.

They've taken our power.
We're afraid of slavery.
We're afraid of guns.

We're afraid of the police.
Fields of violet wildflowers flash
through train windows.

The man pushing the snack cart
grew up in those fields.
His pale-jade gaze hits you.

You stare back.
You share his understanding
of defeat yet you smile anyway.

What has been created
wishes you both weren't
created.

READING

Kiss me on the bus up the mountain.
The air conditioner is broken.
We sip green bottles of orange blossom water.
You say we're *crazy-crazy-crazy*.
You're from the south but live in the big-white city.
You see the south in me   the big
white-city's blue radiation.
We should be in blue   swathes
of it   a tent of it beneath cobalt.
My hand through your coils as you sleep
as I read the green   the black of you.

HER YELLOW DRESS

I loved a woman who wore
a yellow dress but not the woman
within eyeshot. The one

on the tiled street pointing at the
post office is not the one I loved.
Perhaps she knows me?

Has read my name somewhere?
Has seen my photograph among
other photographs   acquaintances of friends?

The way she sways. The dress sways
about her. I'm thinking of another woman.
The woman I knew years prior   her

glowing self in that perpetual gray.
My grayness scorched away.
Love   rain   love in the rain.

The yellow dress in waves near us.
We glistened.
Hawks watched.

We gawked at hawks.
We gawked at each other.
The yellow of her dress

surrounding her face.
Something seen in Florence.
Something I stood before   weeping.

Weeping through that room.
I stood before her weeping.
Alessandro she said leaving

the gallery   bells of sunlight over us.
Taleggio   radicchio
on crescia   wine grassy in glasses.

They murdered him.
Wound him in a rug so few would
see him dead in that city.

There was yellow thread
in the wool carpet   the same yellow
as her yellow dress.

The same yellow in the painting
I continue to see.
The same yellow of a bridge

we crossed licking
cones of lemon gelato.
Why am I thinking of her?

Our defeat?
Our vanishing?
What we declared to limestone   to

fields profuse with life   not alive.
Not here.
Nothing here

but gray.
This void   I declare
this void.

SOMETIMES I BELIEVE I'M A MOROCCAN POET EXILED ON MARS

But I'm from the middle of another country.
My cells are snow crystals with faults perpetually
breaking   fusing to others.
I see red   violet in an opal sky.

In autumn   the pies are pumpkin   cherry.
But for nine years I've written poems
near seawater   on beaches where
camels graze longing not to see seas.

But I want to see them.
Not storms swirling pages to ash.
So much red moving clockwise   counter.
Where are the clocks? Time as pastoral.

The budding   bursting   the flight
of seeds   the spheres of hay
wound on land purged.
But all I see is dust   my hand in dust.

I'm writing in dust.
What I'm writing will become dust.
I'm the premonition
of dust exiled here.

MR. COLTRANE   IT'S AUTUMN
IN THESE MOUNTAINS

But the black cat stares aureate from the drying catalpa.
The remaining leaves are nets unable to hold

what they were. Preservation   experience
induced mincing what used to be mighty   what

used to lark at weakness.
But you can't hold that self   its

purity   sumptuousness no longer.
You see a black coat. Someone

is wearing a black
coat as his indigo-eyed dog

rolls in collapsing leaves.
In that air   something

is overripe. Something is dying.
You can't hold that self

in these mountains.
The rough-rough of them as you

transfigure inside a song. As you praise
what you have found.

Glory to its grace.
Glory to its grace.

You see it in hands   on
thistles flowering mauve.

The gold earth   that
gold in you is a dog barking.

It needs to run.
It needs to roll in collapsing leaves.

MUSICIANS IN RED: A SUMMONING

Red in the red in the red in
the way they summon the unseen.
The way the unseen takes   we see.
Always seeing the taken.
We're moaning as a chorus.
Its treachery drips from strings   bangs
against iron.
A wife writhes   then another   then
another   then a prostitute   then
a philosopher recalling her daughter.
They're taken by the unseen.
They don't see their motion.
Faces to red rugs   hair charged with static.
Bullets pilfer the back of a black boy.
His family name refers to a garden
or the thing a garden gives.
This seen because
we line the streets.
A red flag hangs on the wall.
They're wearing billowing red.
The youngest leaps   then again.
There's bliss in his leaping.
His ability to take what
is high   the unreachable   to
touch it   glory.
It's glory that makes them writhe.
The police gather outside.
Incense for the writhing women   for
the sky above that roofless place.
We're unseen until we're not.
Until we're taken   that

sound of taking.
How many times?
Our chorus.
They're coming inside to take.
Many are coming.
Many unseen.
Some seen.
Many are seeing.

DUSK INTO DAWN: THE RIPPLING

for the mine workers of Jerada

Oh moon   you overwhelm in your wideness.
The clay roofs don't overwhelm as they cut
red triangles into sky   into you as sheep graze.

I'm a witness to bullion light   a witness
to a calm not really itself.
I know the explosion   feel its sulfuric holes.

We're crushed in holes.
The caving in of what we've
hollowed   that initial snap inaudible.

What we've made is without stability.
Wide red flags   we're marching
with red flags rippling as the waiter's

eldest son kisses his cheek.
His youngest reaches for his ears.
He has served two men roasted meat.

They're smoking   speaking through their smoke.
One of their eyes is that moon.
Colossal   strange   unseeing

yet beautiful. Its red cuts ripple.
All over this place the rippling   the call
to ripple that which is still.

BLUE OVER BICYCLES

I'm following you on a newly built
road   one of setts   their borders
slightly detached.

Our clothes are several blues like the sea
that is near but we can't see it.
I see myself lifting my hand hoping

to meet yours as the wheels of our
bicycles continue their whirl.
But I don't want to fall   to tumble   to be tattered.

I dissolve myself into myself   blue
into blue into air. We're euphoric
on this road suddenly yellow.

You speak of another's betrayal.
He shook for days smelling her vetiver.
He howled as swifts spat their nests.

I'm betraying myself silently   a
lightning of neurons.
Clementine trees used to grow here.

I used to ride my bicycle until dark.
Until my mother shouted my name into
blackness   into the clattering leaves

of red maples. If I don't say it here   I
will in the mosque   knees to
carpet   forehead to carpet.

My name   my hollow name.

FOLLY

Compare your proximity to blackness to hers.
You say she's closer.
That she's not of this country.

She claims Brazil because you've
taken the country she knows   the only
one   its mosques   loquat trees.

She claims that version of blackness
because it seems safe.
Because it's supposed to be pretty.

Because it was meant to dissolve.
We're walking on the beach.
I speak of the calling I hear from the sea.

A summoning home of someone distant.
We're watching England play Sweden.
You say there's a player like you   one

like me on the Swedish team.
But I thought no one was like us?
I'm black. No proximity   I solely am.

I was once in Lisbon watching a family toast
the looming marriage of a daughter.
Her Brazilian mother was black   Afro dyed blonde.

Her father was white with no hair.
Their daughter's fiancé was white.
They clanked glasses of beer   strings

of white bubbles formed white foam.
As a girl   her mother was obsessed
with Brocos' painting.

She watched ink dissolve in water.
She wanted to dissolve in the sea.
Did she pass this folly to her daughter?

Did your friend see the same painting?
Feel it at home   school   in the air
when straightening her hair?

Does she wish to dissolve in you?

FOR ROUNDNESS

You were buying balloons   two
of them beneath the sycamore.
The young seller wondered why.

One of them eating a granola bar
as he watched you pull change from
your goatskin wallet. The one you

bought in Warsaw the month
young women wore gray felt hats.
The men who rioted

were bald   crazy   hated themselves
more than the ones they claimed to hate.
But you were buying balloons

because they were round   something
like planets or the self fully
itself after a life of malformation.

You'd almost given in to
the blow   dizziness   maliciousness.
But that was too easy. Falling into it.

You've traveled doming
dents to cathedrals.
You step away to buy your two friends balloons.

When they ask why   you say *it is summer.*

JAWAD'S FLOCK IN MOHAMMEDIA

A patch of sunlight on the wall   thin shadows
like worn nets or the snagged stockings
of a voracious lover impair that patch.

Our shoes tap the marble stairs down-down.
The flock suddenly silent.
But I heard them last night.

Thought I heard them but the packed train
that evening may have induced delirium.
I stood for five hours flattening myself

on dirty windows so the beggars could pass.
But I'm begging for that sound now   the pensive
parakeets in steel cages.

Who's the stranger smelling of lake   shells?
The only named bird is white hiding
in a wood box with spotted eggs.

That sound so much like the breeze
against palm fronds in the park where we walked.
I saw azure parakeets flying

to the severed steeple then to you.
What returns to the broken?
What circles about that which beats?

The solitary so against that flock
flapping as if one being.
We're against it.

We're the solitary moving in solitude.
The wind surrounds.
Later your hands through her hair

as the flock circles near the ceiling.
You circle her.
They're circling as they sing.

Sunlight over everything.
You're waiting for another song.

NEITHER ATLANTIC NOR MEDITERRANEAN

after Salah Ettajani

Pretend this sea is tepid.
Pretend I'm not being pushed
to where I don't want to be.

The fight to be   to breathe where I want.
I'm splashing.
Circles widen until they are not.

They're lines
now that bend.
I'm in line waiting for what

they'll give.
Not this. Not this blue thing.
I'm destroying it.

They see me destroying it in the street.
Dianthus   swiftly.
Someone will offer my grandfather dianthus.

PERFORMANCE DAY IN THE VAULTED THEATER

for my former Moroccan students who are creative

Because this is an ending   they
stand in the stage's center.
One at a time they read alone.

Dust as aura in subdued light.
Pin-lights in the ceiling like
planets in red space.

This is what you've created.
Made into something space-like
in a place insisting on boundary   eyes

to the floor. You have washed rice   green
beans   peeled carrots   toasted pine nuts.
You've soaked dried cherries in pomelo juice.

You've prepared the rice salad   that
signifier of ending   that tradition.
You're leaving this place.

Recalling its conflict.
The love you passed   you felt
in that room   at that square table.

Now you sit in a red chair
watching them sit in red chairs
watching what they've

made   wrought
into being   bloody   fresh.
This new vast space we see.

We're roaming   speaking in it.
Farewell to locks   the snapping
grasp of steel. This theater is for play.

We're playing.
We're able to play.
We're making what we are.

THE SPACESHIP IN TAMRI

Above it was a sign welcoming refugees   a poster
of Sonny Rollins blowing the world into another.
The roof is gone   burned away
so it could land where it could.

The aliens we are recognize its jeweled
lights   its saffron smoke.
Save us from this relentlessness
as our armor flakes.

What we make   makes this place burn.
Our joy of burning joy into atmosphere
but this air isn't owned by the joyous.
Something other rules   claims possession

of what we breathe   the rays on our skin.
We're practicing song
with saxophone   drum   something
stringed   jeweled   as olive branches thrash.

We have wept in Florence.
Have reddened in Chinguetti.
Have understood this place as merely itself.
But save us from this.

That afternoon   the fish was cooked
with cauliflower. Eaten with torn
bread   green oil that smelled of rosemary.
The fisherman smelled rosemary in wind.

He saw the sky burning.
The red village burns.
Save that which burns.
Save us from their burning.

AUBADE: TROPOSPHERE

I'm mourning what will be lost.

These crystals over us   a castle's

ephemeral shine. This is

what the troposphere makes.

We're watched by something other than eyes.

We see ourselves as beings sprung from river rocks.

We're the only ones aware of a particular

chill   the necessity of relentless return.

The café where we decide to wait doesn't close.

The medicine bottles on each table

hold a single ranunculus.

You speak of its rhythm.

Its persistence despite uproot   cutting   cold.

This moment will not survive the constant tug.

I see it.

Oh love   look.

ADORATION

Dogwoods were adored by
Adam because they could be seen   distinguished
without ample effort. Their blossoms matched houses not yet built.
Never would they've needed building if temptation hadn't been so luscious.

TACHFYN'S CATS

The runt has barely one eye.
She stays in your hand unafraid of its
closing   the cruelty everywhere.
The cruelty she knows you know.
The liquid cruelty you trust every day   you test.
The heaving   the brine   the starfish
it flings to sand. The women
it returns naked   bloated   dead.
Your fingers are stained
with mackerel tinned in oil.
Your cats are eating mackerel in front
of your door in the
city   behind the rage of water
professing to them   you.

Drink tea with the stranger who brings
walnuts   raw almonds.
Show him photographs of your father
when he was your age.
Show him photographs of the woman
you'll live with   the house you'll buy
in a beach town crowded with goats.
The stranger is obsessed with mirrors.
He thinks you're your father.
He is his father.
The mineral in your irises is the same
in that cat's   gold   anomalous.
You watch gold in the waves
with the stranger.

Nothing is settled.
We live   then again   then.

REFLECTING

The deaf speak with lashing hands.
Their thoughts explode through
fingers   wands with invisible shock.
One of them notices the boys bringing

their girlfriends sticks of bread in foil packages.
The girls' reflections on the foil   not what
they saw that morning in their mirrors.
But older   perhaps not them at all

but women they were expected to be.
Women like their mothers alone
in pale rooms waiting for finches
to fly through almost windows.

What is expectation?
She expects the deaf man to speak   to not
stare when she stares.
To turn away when her lover offers dry bread.

Light glints from her lover's
silver chain.
She was once silver.
In that dream   she couldn't hear.

Her mouth flooded with sea.
The fish were mirrors cutting through waves.
Waves of mirrors   waves of fish
as mirrors   they could see everything.

The deaf man folds his hands.
Her lover notices him.
My life.
My life here.

THE ALMOST LIFE

1.

It's time to unlock the theater doors.
You wanted to let everyone inside
to see what had been abandoned. The Moors
flickering on screen. So much dust inside
that building you have made into a life.
Charming the depression of poverty
holding hostage the rhythm a god might
jolt   make obsolete if the lottery
were won. You're holding the giant paper check.
You can fund young filmmakers. Renaissance
in this sea town   free town they assumed wrecked.
But you're built from wreckage. Madly ensconced
to what they see as ruin. You hate fools.
Let them die. In death they will find fresh rules.

2.

Let them die. In death they will find fresh rules.
You are confident of this shrewd knowledge
because you've been close. On the brink where ghouls
waited. Puff-puff-puff near sea astonished.
You were told they'd appear as hyenas.
You were told they'd appear in the desert.
Take you somewhere olive   an arena
as oasis to be devoured   blurt
your name with zeal. But they left boney   gray
as the wet rocks. You were left to live. You
felt that freshness   that breath of heather way
down. That bloody lighthouse beam   skin imbued.
Let this renaissance persist with finches.
In Darwish's park we read on benches.

3.

In Darwish's park we read on benches.
The fisherman hacks a shark into steaks.
The shark's eyes are black. You watch. He clenches
seeing his own eyes   the marbles they'd make
if they'd roll. That breaking sound in the fish
market. We are violating waves   foam.
You watch innards slip to the floor   that squish
of what is hidden exposed to the loam.
You chop vegetables   pepper the shark   smash
garlic as the sea churns brown. Too much wind
today but friends will come for supper. Ash
trees will lose leaves   branches. But they will mend.
You will mend yourself. Gordon plays "Star Eyes."
What does he see? What does he recognize?

4.

What does he see? What does he recognize?
Your country is collapsing without you
there. He left it   away from it   advise
that wanderer   turner away of brew.
Gone from family is gone from the well.
How will you live without water? Salty
sea is all you see. But you'll hear the bells
of the only church. The Christians' faulty
habits will not faze. Water is within.
Splash within it. Drink to remember who
you are among gypsy moths   dust of kin
on their wings. You are here among this blue
not crumbling but caressed by that which builds.
You understand how this life must be built.

5.

You understand how this life must be built.
Find her obsessed with film   obsessed with you.
She adores white walls   blue shutters. Feels guilt
when paint fissures. She admires your stew
offering sage bread wrapped in white paper.
This protects from ghouls. She says. *Have you seen*
them? You ask. *We all have. They aren't vapor*
but beings among us. This knowledge gleaned
among shadows   one finch through the window
singing of what she has seen. What will you
see with her? Might you become her hero
in that city? Gallant among yews
so haughty? *Choose me in this tiny place.*
Please? We must accede this glorious grace.

6.

Please? We must accede this glorious grace.
A filmmaker fills a room with tulips.
On the white beach you play soccer embraced
with salt. Your friends are loud. You feel foolish
yet joyful darting about the sand. Moors
flickering on the beach. She is filming
this with a tulip in her mouth. Brochures
of the film festival heaped then reeling
about the beach   about the players lost
in their bustle   in marine melody
you perpetually hear. Something soft
in their sight of auburn sky   clarity
in stillness. They rest on watery sand.
Renaissance   we carry tulips in hands.

7.

Renaissance   we carry tulips in hands
as this is glorious. The show of what
is possible here where drunks beg in clans.
Where boys recite the Koran   eat walnuts
to maintain their minds. Renaissance as love
of a place you've vowed sustenance. You see
what you have learned. So much to unlearn   doves
cooing in the park. You serve goat cheese   brie
    figs   grapes   almond cookies. You kiss her cheek.
Two filmmakers are encouraged to New
York City. Say they're leaving this antique
life. *But remember this one has made you.*
This land   these visions in this land   these centaurs.
It's time to unlock the theater doors.

THE WATER MY LOVE

I've considered the fort on that steep hill.
The sounds of falling water into itself.
The greenness of algae   moss
growing on the marble basin.

We've walked in a city overrun
with green vines. Now
I'm not in that country.
The breeze is damp.

I'm walking among statues   baroque
rhododendrons.
I see loquats lurid in trees.
Last year   you washed several.

Gave them to me damp
in my palms saying   *Eat.*
I've eaten myself until
barely myself.

Longing for what has gone.
Among ferns   marigolds   I
see you asleep.
My hand is on your forehead

to see what you see.
We're walking down the hill   my hand
at the core of your back.
You say   *Out of dream.*

Now on the train   our hands
warm in the other's as you sleep   as
I notice the graffitied neighborhood   jeans
thrashing against brick walls.

The jeans are the same blue as water.
We're water on that train
holding together what could
detach   what could

roll into something else   into
the street to die.
I'm writing this in a café named
for a Brazilian woman.

The waiter who serves cod
croquettes   coffee
was born in Angola.
I am what I am

whatever I am.

THE WHEELS THEN SEAGULLS

Recall the dead beneath us.
The carriage wheels roll over asphalt
smashing horse droppings as an excessively
perfumed   excessively besuited man

passes on his way to an abysmal job.
The crowned woman leaves
the carriage to sing.
Her mouth aims to sky.

We heed.
Sit in the street where
she stands until midday.
She leaves   palm

cupping her throat.
Something about sea in her mind.
Something about walking into it.
Something about hearing seagulls.

Something about singing to them.
Something about their splashing.
Something about skin in their beaks.
Something about returning.

ODE TO TANGLE

Song sparrows flock above the elms

in circles   inside of circles.

I'm inside of myself circling

that which seems shapeless   senseless   an

inscrutable labyrinth.

What do the elms know of love?

I ask because I know nothing of it.

Yet I'm here struggling in its violence.

The twisted boughs tangle into each

other as I tangle into you.

Not my hands   but my life.

Not the feathers   but the flight.

FAREWELL MOUNTAIN

Going up the mountain   you notice
the green neon surrounding that holy
place   that strip of aspiration
never abandoned. It's almost dark
but you see the gilded
grain fields then a gilded sphere
dangling from a woman's ear.
She's next to you.
She's telling someone over the phone
not to leave. The olive trees are jagged.
You're thinking of swords going
in   opening a thing without wounds.
You feel the sting   the jolts.
Silence is agony within the agony.
The bus wheels hit every pothole
on that newly paved road.
You're weeping for what you must give up.
You pass a town where everyone
appears green neon.
The streetlights are green.
The apples they harvested are green.
The café televisions blaring football
cascade green over rapt faces.
What you've wrought will remain.
They told you this in cluttered
rooms   beneath chandleries   angel's trumpets.
When they were brave to speak   they
were given two decades of confinement.
You're not confined.
You're leaving.
Back to a place moving backward.

That fool   his foolish followers are destroyers.
Burn it all. Burn it all down.
You foresee ruins like those here.
What was almost   pulverized.
But you're not ruins.
You're placing limestone against itself.
So many blocks   fragments   the making
   the making.

TO THE LINEAR

You lead me to that place
where addicts give themselves up.
I have given myself to the linear   to
the straight line.

No longer turning.
No longer considering
that which could
have occurred.

I'm a rocket blasting into
the unknowable.
No more pondering   forever
heavy   forever sick with it.

No longer booming fados.
Or sitting in rooms with suicidal
guitarists plucking sunrise.
No more addiction among addicts.

I'm confessing this to them.
They're moaning.
They're asking me to leave.
I leave you here.

Notes

"Aurora Americana": This poem is set in a small town in Michigan's Upper Peninsula. It begins on the eve of November 7 and ends at the dawn of November 8, 2016. There are four voices: an antebellum black doll, a 45 supporter/voter, an imagined Central Park Five member, and his very young daughter.

"The Jester Lives in the Pale House Built by Slaves": The bronze bust of Martin Luther King Jr., now in the White House, on loan, was made by the artist Charles Alston. In 1806, a black child was born at the White House to an enslaved couple.

"The Slur during Ramadan": Ahmed Zaki (1949–2005) was a darker skinned major Egyptian film star.

"Her Yellow Dress": *Alessandro* refers to Alessando de Medici (1510–1537).

"Musicians in Red: A Summoning": Antwon Rose II of East Pittsburgh, an unarmed seventeen-year-old, was shot in the back, elbow, and face by police officer Michael Rosfeld. Rose died. Rosfeld was acquitted.

"Folly": Modesto Brocos y Gómez (1852–1936) was a Spanish-Brazilian artist best known for his painting *A Redenção de Cam* (*Redemption of Ham*).

"Farewell Mountain": After organizing and participating in peaceful protests in northern Morocco, asking for social and economic fairness and opportunity, specifically in this region, Nasser Zefzafi and other activists were sentenced to twenty years in prison.

Acknowledgments

The Baffler: "The Champions," "The Spaceship in Tamri"
Baltimore Review: "No Longer"
Barely South Review: "City of Saudade"
Bennington Review: "The Moth in the Dryer"
The Café Review: "The Emperor of Terracotta Roofs Confronts the Jester," "Farewell
    Mountain," "Tachfyn's Cats," "To the Linear"
Connotation Press: An Online Artifact: "Reflecting"
Cream City Review: "Sometimes I Believe I'm a Moroccan Poet Exiled on Mars"
Green Mountains Review: "The Turning," "Levitation"
jubilat: "Fanon in Tunis   after Tunis"
Michigan Quarterly Review: "For Roundness," "Fanon's Country," "Gaza Ghazal:
    Blue Dissent," "The Wheels Then Seagulls"
Mizna: "The Slur during Ramadan"
Nimrod: "Performance Day in the Vaulted Theater," "Blue over Bicycles"
Poem-a-Day (Academy of American Poets): "Solemnity"
Poet Lore: "This Scheme of Making," "Canceled Flights: An Odyssey," "Before Dusk:
    The Rippling" (now "Dusk into Dawn: The Rippling")
Portland Press Herald: "Impossibility"
Prairie Schooner: "The Rage: 11 August 2017," "Pastime," "On Valentine's Day a
    Pool in Aleppo," "Blue Neon," "Missiles"
Rhino: "Mr. Coltrane   It's Autumn in These Mountains"
River Styx: "Miss Algeria after Viewing *The Battle of Algiers*"
Ruminate: "Aubade: Troposphere"
Salamander: "The Panther in Lisbon"
Transition: "Americana: A Becoming"
Washington Square Review: "Fanon's Banania 1953"
West Branch: "Ode to Tangle"
World Literature Today: "Jawad's Flock in Mohammedia"

The epigraph for this book comes from *Regarding the Pain of Others* by Susan Sontag
(Published by Farrar, Straus and Giroux. Copyright © 2003 by Susan Sontag). The
quote by Paul Éluard is from an unidentified source and possibly apocryphal.

The epigraph of "Aurora Americana" is an excerpt of "At a Lecture" from *Collected Poems in English* by Joseph Brodsky. Published by Farrar, Straus and Giroux.
Copyright © 2000 by the Estate of Joseph Brodsky.

The epigraph of "Fanon in Bethesda" is an excerpt from a Letter to Roger Tayeb
by Frantz Fanon, dated December 1961.

The epigraph of "The Champions" is an excerpt of "Fear of a Black France" by
Grégory Pierrot from Africa Is a Country (africasacountry.com), July 9, 2018.

Printed in the USA
CPSIA information can be obtained
at www.ICGtesting.com
JSHW082307270823
47227JS00005B/5

9 780691 250571